WHAT PEOPLE SAY
ABOUT STORYMAZE

'Mixes feral cartoon strips with pages of text
in an irreverent science-fiction adventure ... and
provides consolation for readers of any age
who are mourning Douglas Adams.'
Jenny Pausacker, the *Australian*

'I recommend this book to people who have
a slightly warped sense of humour and want
to have a bit of fun with their reading.'
Cameron, aged 13, Canberra, *REACT*

'Jokes, puns and allusions come as fast as the hot
links ... not for the linear narrative luddites.'
Australian Review of Books

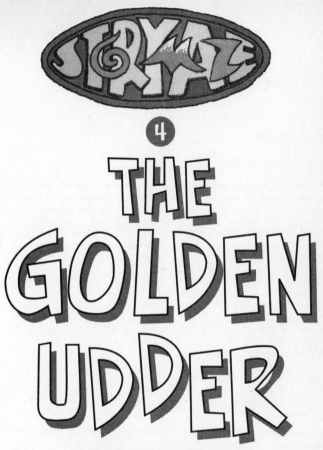

4

THE GOLDEN UDDER

written and illustrated by

TERRY DENTON

ALLEN&UNWIN

FOR KRISTEN

First published in 2002

Allen & Unwin
83 Alexander St
Crows Nest NSW 2065
Australia
Phone: (61 2) 8425 0100
Fax: (61 2) 9906 2218
Email: info@allenandunwin.com
Web: www.allenandunwin.com
Visit Terry's website at: www.terrydenton.com

National Library of Australia
Cataloguing-in-Publication entry:

Denton, Terry, 1950– .
  The golden udder.

  For children.
  ISBN 1 86508 784 X..

  I. Humorous stories – Juvenile fiction. I. Title: (Series: Storymaze; 4).

A823.4

Cover and text design by Terry Denton and Sandra Nobes
Set in Helvetica by Sandra Nobes
Printed in Australia by McPherson's Printing Group, Maryborough, Victoria

10 9 8 7 6 5 4 3 2 1

1

WELCOME!

Sit down and relax.
The story is about to start.

The beginning is a bit complicated, but it's nothing someone with your intelligence and good looks can't handle. If you have read *The Wooden Cow*, you will already know what you need to know. But if you haven't, I will need to tell you some important stuff.

The most important thing is that I am your Narrator. I will guide you through this book. Any questions, don't hesitate to ask.

The second most important thing is that three months ago, Nico, Claudia and Mikey accidentally travelled four thousand years back in time to Ancient Friesia and met a bloke called Ulysses. Ulysses had done a deal with a trickster from the Underworld called Hamish McHaggis so that Queen Chateaubriand, the Queen of Friesia, would marry him. In return,

Ulysses was to steal for McHaggis the sacred icon of Friesia, the Golden Udder.

Foolishly, Ulysses asked Nico, Claudia and Mikey to deliver the Golden Udder to McHaggis, but they got distracted and instead brought it back to Ithaca.

Did they realise how precious this Golden Udder was and what trouble it would cause? Of course not, the fools! They should have asked me.

When the Queen discovered her Udder was missing, she went ballistic. Wouldn't you? She refused to marry Ulysses unless he returned the Golden Udder. He was heartbroken and has been travelling through space and time ever since, searching in all the forgotten corners of the universe for four thousand years, or three months, or both.

That's the story so far.

Now Ulysses is standing outside a burger bar on Ganymede, looking in through the window. He is smiling.

Why is he so happy?

Inside the burger bar are Nico, Claudia, Mikey and M.I.T. They were feeling hungry on their way home from a surf comp on Tantalus and dropped in to Ganymede for a quick snack.

'OK, barnacle-brain,' says Claudia, 'let's get this over and done with.'

'Now, what will I have?' Nico wonders out loud, looking at the menu board.

'Well, seeing there are Haggis Burgers, Haggis Burgers, Haggis Burgers and nothing else but Haggis Burgers on the menu, and this is the only take-away on the whole of Ganymede, I suggest you have a Haggis Burger, granite-head.'

Do you get the impression that Claudia hates Nico?

Nico does sometimes. But then he reminds himself that deep down Claudia really loves him and wants to spend the rest of her life slavishly devoted to him, kissing him, adoring him, having his children and washing his dirty dishes.

Ha! Ha! Ha!

Actually, that's just one of Nico's pathetic fantasies.

In fact, Claudia really thinks Nico is a turkey-brain and wouldn't mind feeding him into an industrial wood chipper and spreading his chopped up pieces over somebody's auntie's garden.

But that's another story.

2

'**BBBUUURRRPPPPPP!!!**' Nico finishes his burger with a flourish.

'About time,' says Claudia. 'You were holding that burger so long I thought you'd bonded for life.'

'Not with the *burger*, I haven't,' Nico thinks, wistfully looking at Claudia.

They leave the restaurant. Do they put their rubbish in the bins thoughtfully provided by the management so that when the next customer sits down the table will be clean?

No, of course not.

They walk through the carpark and wander into a dark alley. I always tell heroes in stories I narrate never to go into dark alleys at night. But do they ever take any notice?

Predictably, they are attacked. They are overpowered, blindfolded and taken a short distance away. In the process M.I.T. is thrown against a wall and sat on by Mikey. Poor M.I.T.

When the blindfolds are removed, Ulysses and two Friesian heavies stand over the

Ithacans. They are in a dark, empty warehouse.

'The Queen of Friesia is very angry,' says the heavier of the two heavies. 'She wants us to rip out your hearts and feed them to the dogs.'

'Cut off your ears and pull your brains out through your nostrils,' says the lighter heavy.

Nico looks at Ulysses. 'What's going on? I thought we were friends.'

'We are, Nico,' says Ulysses. 'But this is love.'

'You love me?'

'No, that would be tragedy,' says Ulysses. 'It's the Queen of Friesia I love. I want to marry her, but something's come between us.'

'Me?'

'Not you, Nico – the Golden Udder.'

'Oh, that!'

'You were meant to deliver it to Hamish McHaggis. What happened?'

'Oh, that was Claudia's fault,' says Nico, embarrassed.

'**My fault?**' shouts Claudia.

'Well, it is lucky you didn't give it to McHaggis, Claudia,' says Ulysses. 'Then it would have been lost forever. And my happiness with it.'

'So was Hamish McHaggis angry?' asks Claudia.

'Yes, but there was nothing he could do,' says Ulysses. 'The Queen is a powerful woman. She called in a few favours and the gods ordered him back to the Underworld. But, tell me, is the Golden Udder safe?'

'Don't worry, Ulysses,' says Nico. 'At least *you* will be lucky enough to marry your true love. The Golden Udder is in my beach box on Ithaca.'

'Then as long as the Golden Udder is safe, you are safe,' says Ulysses. 'And my Queen will be so happy.'

'Have we ever let you down before?' says Nico. There is a long silence.

'Yeah, OK. Well, we won't this time,' says Nico.

Ulysses watches as the Ithacans walk up the dark alley, despite the wise warnings from a concerned Narrator. They grab hold of M.I.T. and form an image of their favourite beach.

'See you in Ithaca,' calls Ulysses.

'To Ithaca.'

PLIK!

3

Did you know there are quite complex circuits in M.I.T.'s brain, which enable him to carry out his difficult space/time travel functions? The sort of circuits that damage easily if he is involved in a fight, thrown against a wall and then sat upon by a slightly overweight, rhino-headed human?

How badly is M.I.T. hurt? Only time will tell. But the damage doesn't have to be great for our heroes to be sent a long way off course. Do they realise the danger in using a faulty M.I.T.?

Of course not. And I'm not going to tell them. They'd never listen to me anyway.

PLIK!

4

Amazingly, M.I.T. brings them home right on target. Literally. They land on the roof of Nico's beach box.

'You idiot!' says Claudia.

Nico's beach box sits in the sand dunes at the back of the beach. His is the one with the red door. And red walls. And a red roof and floor and verandah. Nico likes red. Our heroes climb down off the roof.

'Where did you hide the Udder?' asks Mikey.

'Under my bed,' says Nico.

'You stuffed a priceless Friesian Udder under your bed?' says Claudia. 'What a moron!'

'No problem. You worry too much,' says Nico, stepping into his beach box. 'Everything's under control . . . '

CRASH! THUMP! KERPLUNK!

'Is everything still under control?' says Claudia.

The short answer to that question is no.

Nico is wrestling on the floor with a bloke called Amycus. Have I mentioned him before?

I probably did and you weren't listening. He is one of Nico's old school buddies. They were once great friends and played together all the time, until something happened. Now they do nothing but fight.

Nico has Amycus in a headlock on the ground.

'You were trying to steal my Burke and Wills,' says Nico.

He's right there. Amycus has always wanted Nico's legendary Burke and Wills surfboard. They are rare as hen's teeth. Nico got his from his father, who got it from his mother, who won it in a surf comp. As surfboards go it is the best there is.

'No, Nico, my old friend,' says Amycus. 'I wasn't stealing your board. I was returning it.'

'What?'

'I had to borrow it. I knew you wouldn't mind.

Some bloke challenged me to a surf comp.
I knew I could win with your board.'

'And did you?' says Nico, releasing Amycus.

'Well, no, but he cheated.'

'Ha! You're hopeless, Amycus.'

'No, I'm not. I could out-surf you any day.'

'Yeah, sure.'

'Could!'

'Couldn't'

'Could!'

'Couldn't.'

'And what about the Golden Udder?' says
Claudia. 'Have you seen that?'

'Oh, that!' says Amycus. 'It's gone.'

'What do you mean it's gone?' screams
Claudia. **'Gone where?'** She is holding him by
the collar, nearly choking him.

'I lost it.'

'Lost it?' she says.

'To this bloke called Limousin, in the surf
comp. He wanted the Udder so badly he
challenged me to a comp. He had this brilliant
Braxton-Hicks board. If I won, I'd get the board.
If he won, he'd get the Golden Udder. And me
surfing with your Burke and Wills. I just knew
I couldn't lose.'

'But you did,' says Nico. 'Big surprise!'

'So he took the Udder.'

'I'm going to kill you,' says Claudia.

'No, me first,' says Nico.

'So where did he take it?' asks Mikey.

'To his home, on Santa Gertrudis.'

'Any idea where that is?' asks Claudia.

'Yeah,' says Mikey. 'It's in the Bovine Galaxy.'

For those of you who are interested, look it up in the Map of the Universe in the back of this book. But, hurry back, I've got more story to tell!

'We'll have to go to Santa Gertrudis then,' says Mikey, 'to get the Golden Udder back.'

They take hold of M.I.T.

'To Santa Gertrudis,' says Mikey.

At first nothing happens. Then slowly the Ithacans' bodies begin to disassemble.

PLIK!

They are gone. Their Quest for the Golden Udder has begun.

Poor M.I.T. is still feeling a bit tired and emotional. He disassembles Nico, Claudia and Mikey in the usual way, but when he tries to reassemble them, things go horribly wrong. The god of Chance becomes involved. Sometimes their bits reassemble in a different order, other times in duplicate (or triplicate) and sometimes not at all. They could be sent to two or three different places at the same time or to no place at all.

A neat trick really. We could all use a faulty M.I.T. some days. Imagine: you could be at school and at the beach at the same time. Perfect.

For you, dear reader, this means that you have entered the STORYMAZE and reading this book becomes a bit trickier.

M.I.T. has sent Nico, Claudia and Mikey on two very different paths. And you have to make a choice.

One path is slightly familiar and slightly dangerous. To follow it, read on to Chapter 5, page 13.

The other path is safe, sure and dependable. That's the one I would choose. Read on to Chapter 6, page 18.

Your choice.

5

PLIK!

They M.I.T. out of there, and I suggest you do the same, right back to Chapter 4, page 8, *and choose again.*

6

PLIK!

M.I.T. may look a bit out-of-focus, but his circuits are sharp. He has brought the Ithacans to Santa Gertrudis, right into Limousin's dining room.

Limousin is shocked at first. You would be too, if three and a half people magically appeared on the other side of your table when you were sitting down to dinner.

It takes some explaining, but Claudia eventually soothes the confused Limousin. She also explains their quest for the Golden Udder.

'**You want my Udder?** Why should I help you?' he says. 'What do I get out of it?'

'What can we offer you?' asks Claudia.

Now an amazing thing happens.

As Limousin's food is placed on the table, there is a loud whining noise. Two huge mosquito-like creatures fly through the window straight to Limousin's meal. He explodes with rage.

'You rotten harpies! Will you never leave me in peace?'

These harpies are having a ball. Like jet fighters, they fly around Limousin's head, dive-bombing his meal and covering everything with poo.

Nico watches. He is impressed with their skill and accuracy. Limousin starts swinging his knife and fork at the harpies. But they are just too quick for him.

SPLAT!

NICO TAKES SOME STRING FROM HIS POCKET.

'Sit with me and eat,' says Limousin. 'This
will be my first unpooed on meal for years.

'Allow me to help you,' he continues. 'I did
have the Golden Udder, but lost it in a card
game to a big Zebu, called Simmental. You

must go to Zebu. Tell Simmental I sent you. He might trade the Golden Udder, but he will demand a high price.

'It will not be easy,' he tells them, when they say goodbye. 'To get to Simmental's compound you must pass through the Dreaded Holsteins.'

'Holsteins? What are they?' asks Nico.

'You will see. Your little friend will be powerless there ... '

Mikey looks him in the eye. 'We will think of something.'

Our heroes take hold of M.I.T.

'To Zebu.'

PLIK!

The STORYMAZE gives you a difficult choice here.

I would advise you to turn to Chapter 7, page 22, and forget the other choice.

But if you never listen to the advice of wise Narrators, then go ahead, turn to Chapter 9, page 28, instead. But, remember, I did warn you.

7

'This isn't Zebu,' says Claudia. 'What are you
playing at, M.I.T., you idiot?'

They look around. They are back in
Limousin's dining room. And Limousin can't
believe that they have appeared in front of his
eyes for a second time.

'Back so soon?' he says.

But now he is not looking at the Ithacans.
His eyes are closely watching M.I.T. He figures
he could use a device that can transport him
through space and time so easily.

'Let me see that,' he says.

The Ithacans recognise the look in
Limousin's eyes. They move to the door.

'Guards,' shouts Limousin.

'**Run!**' yells Nico.

The Ithacans flee over the balcony and down
the hill. Limousin's guards chase after them.

The Ithacans don't have enough time to
stop and use the M.I.T. They must keep ahead
of the guards. The path leads through thick
jungle, then up a hill to a clearing and a cliff.

They are trapped.

8

It's a very long and rickety bridge made of
timber and vines. On either side is jungle.
Above is blue sky. Below is a drop of about a
thousand metres into a canyon with a tiny river.

'It's a long way down,' says Nico.

'Just don't look,' says Claudia.

'Oooh, I think I am going to be sick. Can I
hold your hand, Claudia?'

'Oh, sure, and let you puke on it. I don't
think so, somehow.'

'We've got to get off this bridge,' says Mikey.

The bridge suddenly starts to bounce and sway again. Claudia looks up.

'Holy Occhilupo!'

Limousin's guards are running across the bridge towards them. The Ithacans run in the opposite direction. They can't let themselves be captured and lose M.I.T.

CRAAACKK!!!

The rotten bridge timbers break and Nico falls through.

'AAAARRRGGGHHH!!!'

With one hand, Nico catches the bridge cable. But he struggles to keep his grip. He feels so much heavier than normal. And there is a pain in his ankles.

PLIK!

The Ithacans M.I.T. to somewhere. But I am not sure where. I could flick forward a few pages and tell you, but that would spoil it. All you need to know is that the poor damaged M.I.T. brain has misfired again. And that means you have to exercise yours.

There is Chapter 11, page 36, *or* Chapter 13, page 43. *How can you possibly make a choice, I hear you ask? Well, let me make it easy for you. Choose to go to* Chapter 11 *and your life will change forever. Your family will throw you out onto the streets, forcing you to eat rats and spiders and work in a factory cleaning toilets with your tongue.*

Choose to go to Chapter 13 *and you won't be so lucky.*

9

Desperate to catch M.I.T., the Ithacans follow him down passage after passage, turn after turn, ever deeper into the pyramid. Occasionally they catch sight of him in the distance.

Eventually they arrive at a great space where light filters down from above. The room is empty. There is no sign of M.I.T. He must have come in, but how did he get out? There's only one door...

And now that is starting to close!

'Holy Occhilupo!' yells Nico.

They rush for the door, but too late.

SSSHHHH . . . KLUNK!

(That's the sound of the door closing, just in case you were wondering.)

'We're trapped!' says Claudia. 'This is ridiculous.'

'I've seen lots of movies like this,' says Mikey, 'and there's always a way out.'

'This is no movie, you blockhead. This is real.'

'M.I.T. got out,' says Nico, 'so there must be a secret door somewhere.'

They start feeling the walls and the floor, exploring every joint, every crack and every tiny imperfection. There is a section of carved hieroglyphics, and the Ithacans touch and poke and push every part of it. But still no doorway appears.

Mikey slides down to the floor, leaning against the wall. 'Things are crook,' he thinks. 'No M.I.T. No Golden Udder. We're trapped in a sealed room in a pyramid on some loony planet who-knows-where in the universe.'

Nico and Claudia are searching round in the centre of the room, right under the skylight. But where Mikey is sitting the edges of the room are darker. There is a tiny patch of light just a little way across the floor. It is coming from a tiny hole in the stone roof to the side of the main light shaft.

'Hey, look at this,' he calls to the others.

Nico looks at the floor.

'Here's another one.'

'And another.'

Mikey waves his hand over the patch of light and for a moment he breaks the beam.

SSSSHHHH . . . KKKRRRRKKK!

An opening appears in the wall.

Nico blocks out one of the other shafts of light.

SSSSHHHH . . . KKKRRRRKKK!

Another opening appears.

Claudia blocks the remaining beam of light and a third opening appears.

'Which way do you reckon M.I.T. went?' asks Claudia.

'This way,' says Nico, pointing to the opening with stairs leading upwards.

'No, I reckon this one,' says Claudia, pointing to a long passage turning to the left.

Mikey is unsure. He sniffs around a bit, checks the floor for footprints and eventually points to the third opening with stairs leading downwards towards a gloomy darkness.

You, dear reader, cannot stay here. You must follow one of the Ithacans.

To follow Claudia, read on to Chapter 10, page 33.

If you are foolish enough to follow Nico, turn to Chapter 12, page 38.

If you are entirely crazy and choose to follow Mikey, advance to Chapter 15, page 50.

10

'Come on!' yells Claudia, leading Nico and Mikey through the opening. A short way along the passage, they stop. Before them appears a vision of an old woman dressed in rags. She points at them.

'Beware, you seekers of the Golden Udder, for you are entering the temple of the Great One.'

That said she slowly disappears.

'What was that all about?' says Mikey.

'I don't know and I've no time to wonder,' says Claudia. 'We have to catch M.I.T.'

She rushes along the corridor, down a straight section, then up some stairs, around many turns to even more stairs. Ahead there is a doorway. Warily they peer in.

There is a large room filled with a throng of chanting monks. (If that's what a group of monks is called.) The monks turn and throng around the Ithacans and lead them to the front of the room where there is a stone throne. One of the monks gently pushes the Ithacans to their knees telling them to close their eyes.

A bell rings three times. There is a strong whiff of incense. The head monk directs them to open their eyes again and gaze upon the wonder and mystery of the Great One.

The Great One? Just like the lady in rags said.

Before Nico, Claudia and Mikey, in a cloud of incense, stands the Great One. He reaches forward and taps them each gently on the head with a peacock feather. Then in his mighty voice he calls to the visitors:

'**11000.**'

'M.I.T. What are you playing at, you fool?' Claudia yells.

Now M.I.T. is angry. He lets out a stream of digital abuse and points his feather at Nico, Claudia and Mikey.

The monks advance on the Ithacans and start hitting our heroes with peacock feathers. The pain of being hit by one hundred and one peacock feathers is too much for them.

'STOP! STOP!' Mikey yells. 'M.I.T., we are

your friends. We'll do anything, just stop the bopping!'

'Anything?' the head monk asks.

'Anything.'

And so it comes to pass that the Great One, M.I.T., lives and rules in his mountain paradise for a hundred years. And his faithful servants Nico, Claudia and Mikey look after his every whim for the rest of their humble, dreary and sad lives. And they never succeed in their quest for the Golden Udder.

And you, dear reader, will do the same unless you take this opportunity to escape. Go back down the corridor to the great space from which you came and choose another path. But try and get it right this time!

Foolish ones turn to Chapter 12, page 38.

Crazy people advance to Chapter 15, page 50.

11

PLIK!

Sorry! Big M.I.T. misfire.

The Ithacans go nowhere. That means they're still on the bridge.

'**00000**,' says M.I.T.

Twelve of Limousin's biggest and most powerful guards gather around. They reach for Nico's arm.

The vine cables start to strain and crack. Suddenly the bridge gives way.

'**NOOOO!!!**'

They all fall down, down, down, towards the river below.

SPLASH!!

The Ithacans land in the water. It is strangely peaceful and very cold. A few metres away, Limousin's guards splash and flail about trying desperately to keep afloat.

The Ithacans calmly swim towards the bank.

'**No!**' yells Claudia. '**Look!!!**'

The whole bank of the river is covered with bonecrunchers, quietly eyeing off the swimmers.

'We're safer here,' says Mikey, 'they hate water.'

The Ithacans start swimming downstream with the current. They catch up to a log and relax, letting it draw them along.

Limousin's guards are not such good swimmers and have fallen well behind. In fact they now appear to be swimming back upstream. The Ithacans think they have blown them away. Ithacans always think they are the best swimmers in the world.

Around a bend in the river, the current gets stronger. Now the Ithacans can hear a loud, roaring noise.

'It's a waterfall!!' yells Mikey.

In fact, it's a very long drop waterfall – the longest long drop waterfall in the known universe. But they don't know that. They try to swim back up the river, but the current is just too strong and the river too wide. They are swept to the very edge of the waterfall. They plunge over and fall down towards the rocks and a bloody end!

You must act quickly before they are pulverised to death. Go back to Chapter 8, page 24.

12

Nico leads Claudia and Mikey through the doorway. The stairs lead up and curve off to the right. They stop at a landing.

An old man dressed in a pirate suit sits on a plinth.

He beckons to them, whispering:
'Ye seekers of the Golden Udder,
Beware the path to the top
For ye will finish at the bottom.'

He stands up, laughing a wheezing sort of laugh, and shuffles off down the stairs.

Nico looks up the passage and catches a glimpse of M.I.T. in the haze.

39

The Ithacans climb down the outside of the
pyramid and search around the base for M.I.T.
There is no sign of him. No holes in the ground
with tiny legs sticking out. No eyes smashed
like eggs on rocks. No tiny creatures lying face
down in the mud, breathing their last breath.

Nico walks past a pond.

'Pheeeww! What a pong,' he says to himself.
He hears something splashing.

'M.I.T.?' Nico yells.

'101.'

The others come running. Overwhelmed by the smell they stop.

Poor M.I.T. is floating in a sewerage pond hanging on to a piece of wood. Well, it looks like wood.

Claudia and Mikey laugh. They can't help themselves. Of all the places to land in the universe!

'0001.'

'C'mon,' says Nico. 'Stop laughing and help me get him out.'

But Claudia is paralysed with laughter, leaving Nico and Mikey to rescue M.I.T.

They wash M.I.T. in clean water until all traces of sewerage are gone, more or less. (Not that M.I.T. can smell the sewerage, because he doesn't actually have a nose.)

Nico cuddles M.I.T. for a while.

'You smell beautiful now,' says Nico to M.I.T. 'Just like a baboon's bottom.'

'00100,' M.I.T. smiles. Obviously he's never seen a baboon's bottom.

'Come on, you two, we've got to get to Zebu,' says Claudia. 'Let's go.'

They gather around M.I.T.

'Phhheewww!' says Claudia. 'What's that stink?'

'Don't ask,' says Nico. 'M.I.T., take us to Zebu.'

PLIK!

M.I.T. has been thrown against a wall a few times, sat upon, chased by a mad Udder, thrown from the top of a pyramid and dumped into a pond of steaming sewerage, some of which he has swallowed. He is not working at peak efficiency. But there is no other choice – our heroes put their trust in a smelly and confused M.I.T. and so must you.

I would prefer it if you went straight to Chapter 17, page 62.

But if you want to be annoying you could venture off to Chapter 18, page 64.

Your choice. But beware!

13

I'm sorry you had to come here. There is no Chapter 13. I have told you many times it is bad luck to have a Chapter 13 in a book. I will never narrate them. Much too dangerous. Let me tell you why.

Once upon a time, my uncle Rolly was in bed reading a book. As he turned the page to Chapter 13, his bed lamp got tangled with his elbow, fell over and hit him on the head. The lamp had been on for ages so it was quite hot. It burned his head. He screamed and kicked his legs up. Unfortunately his cat was lying on the bed. Uncle Rolly kicked his cat out the open window. Which for most cats would not be a big problem. But Uncle Rolly lived in an apartment on the 18th floor.

The end.

Read on to Chapter 14, page 44 – you'll be so glad you did.

14

45

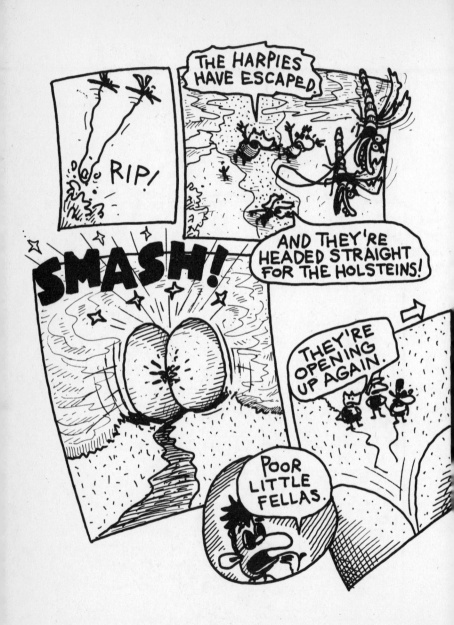

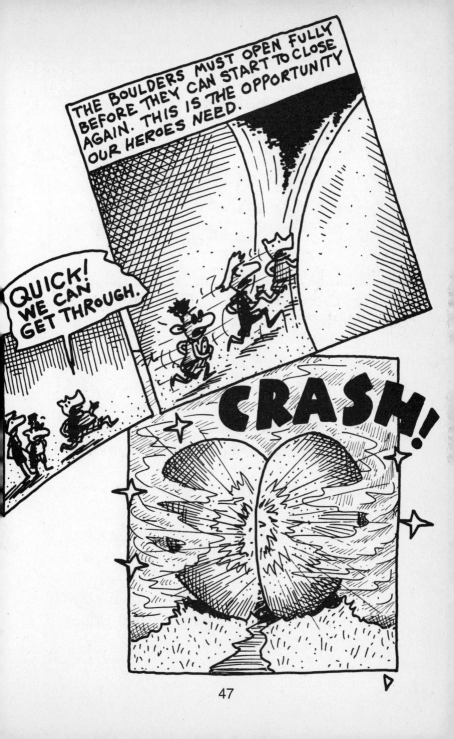

Nico, Claudia and Mikey can't wait to get away from the Dreaded Holsteins. They run down the path, which leads directly to Simmental's compound.

The leader of the Zebus welcomes the visitors but is also suspicious of them.

'We bring you greetings from Limousin of Santa Gertrudis,' says Mikey.

'Aah, my friend Limousin,' laughs Simmental. 'Great man, but a rotten card player.'

Mikey tells Simmental their long story of trouble and woe.

'We are in great danger. Only the Golden Udder can save us,' says Mikey. 'Will you trade it back to us?'

'Your difficult situation has nothing to do with me,' says Simmental. 'I love my Golden Udder and I don't want to part with it.'

'Will nothing persuade you?' says Mikey.

Simmental ponders for a while.

'Well, there is something you could try. Something that no one else has ever achieved. Not even the cleverest Zebu in the land.'

'What's that?' asks Mikey.

'My pride and joy is sick. Perhaps you can heal her.'

'But we are not doctors!'

Simmental leads Nico, Claudia and Mikey down the garden path to a large building. Inside stands a huge and shiny high-speed space sports craft.

'This is my pride and joy, my Space Travellator. She has not worked for seven years. If you get her flying again I will gladly give you the Golden Udder.'

Mikey steps forward smiling.

'Piece of cake!'

What is this piece of cake? Is he going to eat the piece of cake? Is he going to fix the Travellator with a piece of cake?

To find out read on to the incredibly cakey Chapter 16, page 56.

15

MIKEY LEADS CLAUDIA AND NICO
THROUGH AN OPENING IN THE WALL.

51

53

PLIK!

You have escaped from the pyramid. You are extremely lucky. But now you must command the M.I.T. to take you to Zebu and he is extremely dizzy. Take a chance and go to Chapter 14, page 44.

16

'OK, I'll leave you with it,' says Simmental, wandering back to his house.

Mikey hops up into the cabin and tries to start the Travellator. But it is dead. He climbs out again and up the ladder to the engine. He opens the engine hood and starts fiddling around inside. A few minutes later he is humming to himself and making a list of parts.

'I think I know what's wrong, but I have no idea if we can find these things on Zebu.'

Medea, a Zebu servant girl, has been watching Mikey work. She climbs up next to him and looks at the list.

'I know where you can get this stuff,' she says. 'I can help you, if you will help me.'

'How can we help you?' asks Mikey.

'I am sick of being Simmental's servant. If you help me escape from Santa Gertrudis, I will get you the Golden Udder.'

'Sounds good to me.'

'We need to go to the city, to my uncle Ebenezer's store.'

'OK, read me the list,' says Medea.

'Nine reels of high strength copper wire,' says Mikey.

'Easy enough,' says Medea. 'What else?'

'Eight extra-hard rubber grommets, seven large gauge hex bolts, six double-size nappy pins, five holden rings.'

'Check.'

'Four dolly legs, three trench pins, two nurkle plugs...'

'Check.'

'...and a car-fridge element key.'

'A what?' says Nico.

'Do you have any idea what you are doing, Mikey?' asks Claudia.

'Sure,' says Mikey. 'My dad used to have a Space Travellator. We were always pulling it apart.'

'And putting it together again?' asks Claudia.

'Of course,' says Mikey. 'Trouble is they are a bit old now. Parts are almost impossible to find. So we have to improvise.'

They find most of the parts they are looking for in the Zebu city. But there is one part they cannot find anywhere.

'No. 17,' says Medea. 'A Modulator from an Illudium P76 Terrain Vehicle.'

'Holy Occhilupo! What is a Modulator from

an Illudium P76 Terrain Vehicle?' asks Claudia.

'Well, the thing won't work without a Modulator. And we'll never find one from a Space Travellator. So the next best thing is a Modulator from an Illudium P76.'

'So where are we going to get that from?' asks Nico.

'Medea, are there any wrecking yards on Zebu?' asks Mikey.

'No,' she says, 'but my dad used to go to a big one on Fluvium.'

'Ah yes, my dad too. I'd forgotten about that. He always used to talk about a wrecking yard on Planet Fluvium on the other side of the map,' says Mikey. 'If there is a modulator anywhere in the universe, it will be there.'

'And if it isn't?' says Nico.

'Well, have you got any better ideas?'

'What about M.I.T.?' asks Claudia. 'I don't think we can trust him to get us there and back.'

'No choice,' says Mikey.

'To Fluvium.'

PLIK!

Now Claudia has been very unfair to M.I.T. Sure he is a little unwell, but that doesn't mean he can't do his job. Why, some days when you open this book, I have a raging headache, but that doesn't stop me. No way. We professionals can work through the most amazing pain.

So M.I.T., despite his great pain, does his job bravely.

Unfortunately he fouls up badly and sends them to two different places.

So you have to choose between the dark and grimy Chapter 19, page 67, *or the challenging but exciting* Chapter 26, page 98.

   Good luck!

17

PLIK!

Poor M.I.T. Swallowing sewerage must have jammed his circuits. He was supposed to send the Ithacans to Zebu, instead they find themselves plunging down towards a large dam. Can we put this down to clogged circuits, or is M.I.T. being a little mischievous?

SPLASH!

The dam is full of raw sewerage. But Nico, Claudia and Mikey are not screaming and complaining as you would expect them to. Actually they are not quite themselves. When M.I.T. reassembled them he took them back tens of millions of years to an earlier evolutionary form. They have become primitive sewerage eating fish.

That's why they don't scream and complain. They love sewerage. They want to stay here forever. And they will, living happily ever after chewing up other people's waste.

And M.I.T.?

Well, he is free of the Ithacans at last. Not that they care. They are too busy eating their sewerage to notice M.I.T. wave goodbye and wander off happily into the sunset.

And unless you want to spend the rest of your life eating sewerage too, it is time to move on and take Mikey's path.

Turn to Chapter 15, page 50.

18

Actually M.I.T. has reproduced the Ithacans in triplicate and sent them to three almost identical parallel universes. They stand outside three identical doors.

You have three choices:
You could turn to the mysterious Chapter X, page 84.
Or you could visit the explosive Chapter 23, page 93.
Or maybe you prefer the chilling Chapter 26, page 98.

PLIK!
THUMP!
'OUCH!'

Our heroes lie flat on a road, opposite a wreckers' yard.

'Good shot, M.I.T.! This must be Fluvium.'

Mikey crosses the road and rattles the gate.

'Great piles of poo, it's locked!'

'LOCKED!!! Didn't I tell you we should phone first?' says Nico. 'Now what are we going to do?'

Mikey rattles the gate some more. There are about a dozen locks on it. He calls out but there is no response.

'It's getting dark,' says Claudia. 'We've got to do something.'

'Like what?' says Mikey.

'Like break in,' says Medea, pulling out some wire cutters.

'You're amazing!' says Mikey.

Mikey and Medea set to work and soon remove the Modulator from the Illudium's engine.

'Beauty,' says Mikey. 'Now we can get out of here.'

'NOT SO FAST!'

Two guards stand at the bottom of the ladder. They have arrested Nico and Claudia and Medea.

'You will come with us, too,' says the bossy one, whose name is Gordon.

Mikey climbs down and joins his friends.

'Shall we put them in the escape-proof lock-up, Gordon?' says Derek.

'Of course we will, Derek. And then we shall ring the boss and tell him how clever we have been.'

'He will be pleased with us, Gordon.'

'As long as they don't escape, he will, Derek.'

The guards lock the Ithacans up, then call their boss.

'Boss! Yeah, g'day,' says Derek. 'Guess what? I caught some robbers.'

'You, Derek!!!' yells Gordon. 'You caught them!!!'

And while the guards are arguing, the Ithacans and Medea take hold of the M.I.T. and

PLIK!

They leave for Zebu.

Perhaps M.I.T. is starting to feel better, because he lands them right back in Simmental's garage. Pretty soon Mikey is working away on the Space Travellator again.

The problem is mainly to do with the start mechanism. It always is with Space Travellators. Every Narrator knows that. Especially the EH. The engine will go on forever, but the electrics are very dodgy.

'Hand me up the No. 5 sprurkle docker,' Mikey calls to Claudia.

'The what?'

'The No. 5 sprurkle docker.'

'Eh?'

'Here you go,' says Medea, tossing up the sprurkle docker.

'Pass us up the nurkle plugs, too.'

Medea climbs the ladder with a box of parts and starts working with Mikey. They are very careful. One mistake, especially with a P76 Modulator, and they would be looking at a return trip to Fluvium. And by then Ulysses and the Friesian heavies might be getting a little impatient.

Mikey and Medea work well together.

71

Rebuilding a Space Travellator is a job Mikey has done with his father a hundred times before. Out in the garage, 120 degrees below, on the hard concrete floor, rebuilding starter units, cleaning out fusion ports, recalibrating suction clackers and other countless routine maintenance tasks. His dad was a long haul Travellator driver. So keeping up the maintenance was part of the job. Making sure the old EH would go the distance.

Time passes. Have you ever known a time when it didn't? Of course, sometimes it passes more quickly than others. It's all relative. Speaking of which, an hour with Mrs Narrator's relatives seems to last an eternity. But an eternity with my gorgeous manicurist would seem to last only an hour.

Anyway, where was I?

Oh, yes, Mikey and Medea are still fixing the Space Travellator. And Simmental has returned to the garage and is eagerly watching.

'That's it!' says Mikey.

'Well done,' says Medea, playfully punching Mikey on the arm.

'It is finished?' exclaims Simmental.

'Sure is. Get in and try her.'

A smiling Simmental climbs up into the cab and turns the key.

NOTHING!
'WHAT?' yells Simmental.

'Keep your shirt on,' says Mikey, leaning back into the engine and fiddling some more. 'It's OK. It's just one of the nurkle plugs that's come loose.'

He gives Simmental the thumbs up.

'Turn her over again.'

That's techno-talk for 'start it up', which is what Simmental does. This time the engines burst into life and flames blast out of the back of the engine. (Which is a bit unfortunate for a few Zebus, chatting by the exhaust.)

'You beauty!' cries Mikey.

The noise of the engines is deafening.

Tears come to Simmental's eyes. He has dreamed of this moment for years. He gives the Travellator full thrust and it rockets out of the garage into the sky. Terrified Zebus run in all directions.

About an hour later, Simmental returns.

Mikey and Medea clamber up the ladder to the cockpit.

'Good?' says Mikey.

'Fantastic!' says Simmental, smiling.

'Take her for a run.'

'Nah. No time. We have to go, Simmental. We need to take the Golden Udder back to Ithaca.'

Simmental climbs down from the cockpit.

'The Golden Udder?'

'Yes, we must take it with us.'

'Sorry, I can't let you have it. I love that Udder.'

'WHAT?' But we had a deal,' says Mikey.

'That was then. This is now.'

I told you time was relative.

Simmental stands up, towering over the Ithacans.

'New deal. I keep the Udder. You all go away. But thanks for the repairs.'

'You can't do this!' yells Mikey.

'YOU CHEAT!' yells Claudia.

'Well, how do you think I won the Udder in the first place?' laughs Simmental.

'I'll destroy the Travellator,' says Mikey.

But as soon as he moves towards the Travellator, Simmental's guards surround him.

'Take them to the dungeons,' orders Simmental.

Nico, Claudia and Mikey are led away. Medea, meanwhile, slips silently out of the garage.

20

In a damp and dingy dungeon Nico, Claudia, Mikey and M.I.T. sit gloomily discussing their predicament.

'This is another fine mess you've gotten us into, Nico,' says Claudia.

'Me? It was all Mikey's fault.'

'Well,' says Claudia. 'I reckon we should M.I.T. out of here and . . .'

'And what?' says Mikey.

'We don't even know where the Golden Udder is.'

'But I do,' says a voice from the other side of the bars.

It is Medea. She unlocks the door and lets the Ithacans out.

'Follow me.' She leads them past a sleeping guard.

'What happened to him?' asks Mikey.

'Drugged,' says Medea.

'And him?' says Nico as they pass another sleeping guard.

'Drugged, too. I drugged everyone's meal.

That's part of the fun of being a servant. We have half an hour to get the Golden Udder and escape before they all wake up.'

Medea leads them to another room where Simmental himself is slumped in his chair, asleep.

'Him, too?' asks Mikey.

'Ah ha.' Medea smiles.

'Where's the Golden Udder?' says Claudia.

'Follow me.'

Medea shows them through a secret opening behind the snoring Simmental. An underground passage eventually leads to a dimly lit room. In the centre is a mound of what looks, at first, like rubbish. But as their eyes adjust to the dark, it starts to twinkle. This is Simmental's treasure store of gold, money, jewels and other valuables too numerous to mention.

'Beware,' says Medea. 'The treasure is guarded by a fierce dragon.'

CHOMP!

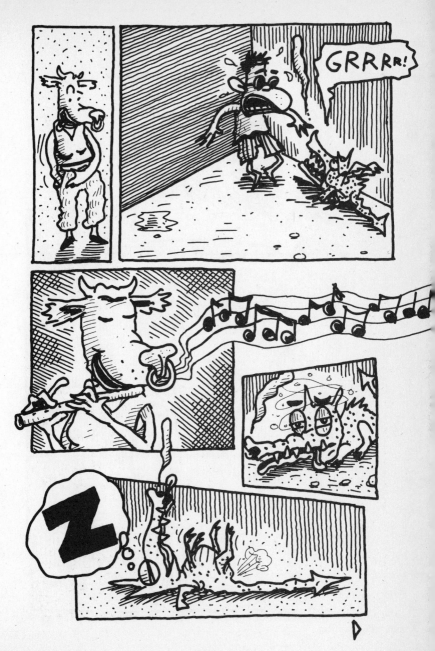

'Quick! We must get out of here,' says Medea. 'The Zebus will soon be waking.'

They hurry back along the passage towards Simmental's room. Now and then Medea stops to look back.

'There's something following us,' she says. 'Take the Udder, Mikey, and wait for me in Simmental's office.'

Then the brave Medea turns and walks back down the passage.

'But . . .' says Mikey.

'Go!' says Medea.

A few minutes later, Medea reappears in Simmental's office carrying the dragon, which doesn't look quite so fierce now.

'He was sick of being locked up underground. I'm setting him free.'

Outside Simmental's house, Medea releases the dragon, which soars off high into the sky, almost out of sight, then returns, flying around their heads, singing a happy dragon song.

Actually it sounds more like someone scraping their fingernails down a blackboard, but to a dragon it must be a happy song.

Now the Zebus are awake and running down the hill after them.

'Bring back my Golden Udder,' screams Simmental.

'We are beaten,' says Claudia.

And she is right, only I didn't want to be the one to tell her that. Before them stand the impassable Dreaded Holsteins and behind them Simmental and his guards. M.I.T. is useless here. Only a miracle can save them.

And sometimes miracles come in strange forms.

Suddenly Medea's dragon rises up and starts flying around her head, singing its strange song. Then it heads straight for the Holsteins.

'NOOOO!' shouts Medea.

The brave dragon flies between the huge boulders, which crash together with an almighty boom. The dragon must surely be destroyed.

'We must go now,' yells Claudia, as the Holsteins start to open up again.

Nico, Claudia, Mikey and Medea rush through the boulders, which crash together again behind them.

'Bring back my Golden Udder!' screams Simmental from the other side of the Dreaded Holsteins. But he cannot get through.

'Poor dragon,' says Medea, looking around in the hope that he may have survived.

But there is no time to mourn, the travellers must keep moving. On this side of the Dreaded Holsteins, M.I.T.'s powers are restored.

They take hold of him and Mikey clutches the Golden Udder tight . . .

'To Ithaca.'

PLIK!

You will have to be quick. Nico, Claudia, Mikey and Medea are speeding back to Ithaca and you'll have to jump to Chapter 27, page 103, *or be left behind.*

Left behind? That's a bit cheeky!

Chapter X

PLIK!

Nico, Claudia and Mikey stand outside the door.

'I think we should go in,' says Claudia.

'Hmm, I have a bad feeling about this,' says Mikey.

'C'mon, Mikey,' says Nico. 'A light in the sky pointing to a stable in a village in the East. We could be part of history here.'

'Two to one, Mikey, we win,' says Claudia, knocking on the door.

It opens a crack.

'How came you here?' whispers a voice from inside.

'We followed the light in the sky,' says Nico.

'What is your quest?'

'We have come to find the Golden Udder.'

The doorman shows the Ithacans inside.

'Igor!' he calls out. 'They are here.'

He ushers the Ithacans into a large room, which looks more like an inn than a stable. It is very light. Claudia and Nico look up to a gaping hole in the roof. Mikey wanders over to the middle of the room. He looks at what has made the hole: a huge bomb wedged into the floor.

'Thank you for coming so quickly,' says a tall man with a fake beard and moustache. 'There's no time to lose. This thing could go off at any moment. Take the tools. We'll leave you to it.'

'But,' says Mikey, 'there's been some kind of mistake.'

The tall man points his gun at Mikey. I'm not sure what kind it is, except that it is the kind that shoots bullets and makes big holes in things. The kind that Mrs Narrator uses to shoot spiders in the toilet.

'You know the password,' he says. 'There is no mistake. Defuse the bomb.'

Mikey has no choice. It's hard to argue with a gun. He steps up to the bomb. Actually he is not as scared as you or I might be if we were asked to defuse a bomb. He knows a bit about bombs. He used to defuse a few with his dad in the garage back home, when they weren't fixing Space Travellators.

Mikey opens up the bomb-case door. Inside there is a mass of wires. This looks much too complex and not at all like the bombs he has played with before. He breaks out into a sweat.

Mikey notices a stripy green wire. He remembers something his dad once told him about stripy green wires in bombs. Mikey takes the pliers and reaches out for the wire.

Sweat pours off his forehead. He can almost touch the green wire. He stretches, he reaches, but his hands are sweaty and he accidentally drops the pliers.

22

CLANK! BING! KRATTLE!

The pliers fall down into the heart of the bomb. And it starts ticking.

Tick! Tick! Tock!

Don't you just love my clever sound effects in this section? We studied sound effects for six months at Narrator School. It was my favourite subject.

Now Mikey sweats even more. So does everyone in the room. And they move as far away from the bomb as possible.

Mikey reaches further into the bomb for his pliers. They must be in there somewhere. He tries to pull his arm back, but now his hand is stuck.

His brow starts sweating like a garden sprinkler. Claudia bravely steps forward with a towel and wipes the sweat away.

'You got any idea what you're doing?' she asks.

'I think so,' says Mikey. 'As long as the oscillator doesn't start tapping we're OK.'

But as Mikey finally wrenches his arm free, a loud tapping noise starts.

Tap! Tap! Tap!

It sounds very like an oscillator.

Then the bomb goes silent.

. . ■ . ! . . . ■ . ! . ! . . . ■ . !

Nobody in the room makes a sound. No one even breathes. The room is so quiet, you could hear a pin drop.

Then, suddenly, a pin drops...somewhere deep inside the bomb.

BOOM!

The bomb explodes. Everyone in the room blows up.

I wasn't expecting the bomb to go off and I blow up too. So does the editor of the book, who heroically throws her body across those of the author and the illustrator in a vain attempt to save their lives. But they are all blown up too. What a mess!

So now you have no choice. With my last breath I have to tell you to close the book.

It is all over.

Evil has triumphed over good.

If you are not happy with that rather messy end to the book, I have taken the opportunity to give you an alternative ending.

I think you should read it. It is better than anything the author could write. And it is yours for no extra cost. Read on to Chapter 23, page 90.

23

(Narrator's alternative, and better,
ending to Chapter 22)

Lets go back to the bit where Mikey drops his
pliers.

CLANK! BING! KRATTLE!

They fall down into the heart of the bomb,
which starts ticking.

TICK! TICK! TICK!

And all the other people in the room scream
in panic and rush out. They don't want to be
blown up. (I know the feeling!)

Of course, Claudia, Nico and M.I.T. stay with
Mikey. There's no way they would leave him at a
time like this. A pool of sweat builds up at
Mikey's feet.

Suddenly the back door opens and in
strides a tall and elegant gentleman dressed all
in black. He steps across to the bomb. Calmly
he reaches down inside and removes Mikey's
hand.

Then he takes out a simple nail file and reaches up to a tiny door high up on the bomb.

Suddenly the ticking of the bomb speeds up.

Tick! Tick! Tick! Tick! Tick! Tick! Tick! Tick! Tick! Tick! Tick! Tick! Tick! Tick! Tick!

That scares the Ithacans. But the-man-in-black stays calm.

Now the ticking of the bomb is so fast it is almost a blur.

The-man-in-black opens the tiny door. Inside is a simple On-Off switch. The brave and fearless man-in-black reaches out with his beautifully manicured index claw and flicks the switch to Off.

The ticking stops.

He closes the door and strides over to the Ithacans, ushering them out the back door and leading them up the dark alley, well away from the inn.

Then he waves farewell.

'But you were magnificent,' Claudia calls out.

'All in a day's work for a Narrator,' he says and strides off into the night.

Suddenly there is a huge explosion.

BOOM!

The inn blows up.

Claudia catches Mikey as he faints and falls to the ground.

'Let's get out of here,' she says.

They take hold of the M.I.T. and . . .

'To Zebu.'

PLIK!

You must hurry, too. There is no time to lose.

Go back to Chapter 18, page 64, *and try another path.*

24

Nico, Claudia and Mikey stand outside the stable door.

'If the Udder in the sky was pointing here,' says Claudia, 'I think we should go in.'

'I'm not sure about this,' says Mikey sitting down on a bench.

'110111.'

'C'mon, Mikey,' says Nico, 'we must go in. Stables in a village in the East. We could be part of history here.'

'We could be history here!' says Mikey, wriggling on the bench. 'We've got to go to Zebu and find Simmental.'

'He's right,' says Claudia. 'We must find the Golden Udder or Ulysses will be after us.'

'So where's M.I.T.?'

'10010,' screams M.I.T. from under Mikey's bottom.

'I must have sat on him,' Mikey says. 'I didn't see him. Honest.'

M.I.T. is looking very crushed – it's been a

bad day for this little microbe. But bravely he shouts out:

'**100000**.'

They take hold of him.

'To Zebu.'

PLIK!

The Ithacans disassemble and disappear.

PLIK!

Unfortunately M.I.T. fouls up badly.

He doesn't send them to Zebu.

In fact, he doesn't send them anywhere.

Or to be more exact, he sends them to nowhere.

They are not even nowhere, really, because that would be somewhere.

In fact, M.I.T. reassembles Nico, Claudia and Mikey so that they are everywhere and nowhere at the same time. Just floating in space.

But even their mothers wouldn't recognise them. Actually, Nico's mother would be happy about that! Their atoms are spread far and wide throughout the universe, floating in a vast endless ocean of atoms.

Look, over there is one of Nico's electrons. And there is a proton from Mikey's leg. And one of Claudia's neutrons is having a chat to a passing electron from the nose of Cleopatra.

So M.I.T. has dropped you and me in it badly, once again. We have reached a dead end.

The best advice I can give you is to read on to Chapter 25, page 96.

25

I'm sorry that you had to come all the way here to find this out, but there is no Chapter 25, unless you care to write it yourself.

The author hasn't had time to do it yet. And I didn't realise it wasn't here. I should have read ahead to make sure, I suppose, but it's not my fault. I'm a busy man.

So you have two choices:

CHOICE NO. 1

Close the book and go to sleep. You know you could do with a good sleep.

And even if you are at school at this very moment, don't worry. Close the book, anyway. Pop your head down on the desk. Stretch out a bit. Make some space. Shove all the stuff onto the floor.

Can you hear that distant, droning sound of cicadas? Well, it's not cicadas, it's your teacher rattling on about something really interesting and you just want to listen. You just want to, but you just . . . you just . . . you just go to sleep.

No one will notice. And try not to give it away by snoring.

Or alternatively, you could try:

CHOICE NO. 2

Go back to Chapter 14, page 44.

Or read on to Chapter 26, page 98 *if you're feeling adventurous. Did I say adventurous? I think I meant stupid.*

26

Nico, Claudia and Mikey stand outside the
stable door.

'Do you think we should go in?' asks
Claudia.

'No, we've got to stay focused,' says Mikey.
'We've got to keep going and find Simmental in
Zebu.'

'That's what I was thinking,' says Claudia.
'We must find the Golden Udder, or Ulysses will
come looking for us. Let's go.'

They take hold of M.I.T.

'To Simmental on Zebu.'

PLIK!

They disappear.

*You will freeze to death too, unless you go back
to Chapter 14, page 44.*

*Go now while you still can. I'll stay here to
make sure everybody gets off the mountain
safely. That's what Narrators do.*

27

PLIK!

M.I.T. returns Nico, Claudia, Mikey and Medea to the beach on Ithaca. They tromp across the sand to Nico's beach box.

Inside, Ulysses and the two Friesian heavies are waiting.

'About time,' says Ulysses, holding out his hands for the Golden Udder.

'We went through hell for this,' says Nico, hoping for a fanfare or some wild applause or just a tiny bit of gratitude.

'I know how you feel,' says Ulysses. 'I've been going through hell without it.'

Ulysses wraps his arms around Nico and they hug.

'Thank you for everything, my friends, but now I must hurry away,' says Ulysses. 'All's well that ends well, eh?'

'I hope it works out well with the Queen,' says Claudia.

'With the Golden Udder in my hands,

Claudia, nothing can go wrong,' says Ulysses. 'I won't keep you any longer, I've got a bride to marry.'

Ulysses and the two Friesian heavies wave farewell and stride off down the beach.

Suddenly Claudia calls out to him: 'Ulysses, you forgot this.' She holds up the Golden Udder.

'I guess I am a bit nervous,' says Ulysses, setting off a second time, the Golden Udder securely under his arm.

'How are you getting home?' yells Nico, but Ulysses is too far away to hear.

Frankly I have no idea how he is going to get home.

28

29

A lone figure sits on beach. It is Mikey. He is writing Medea's name in the sand about three hundred times.

Claudia and M.I.T. walk up and sit down next to him.

'She even knew,' says Mikey, 'what a sprurkle docker was.'

Claudia snorts. 'Sounds like the perfect woman.'

'Now what am I going to do, Claudia?'

'You could try pulling yourself together, Mikey. She's been gone for a week. Snap out of it.'

'Cheers, thanks a lot, Claudia.'

Mikey stands up.

'Where are you going?' asks Claudia.

'I want to be alone,' says Mikey, wandering off into the sunset.

Claudia turns to M.I.T. 'Well, some people just can't take advice,' she says.

'01,' says M.I.T.

THUNK!

110

The Very Last Chapter

And that, dear reader, is the end of our story.

The Golden Udder is back where it belongs on Friesia. Ulysses and the Queen are going ahead with their wedding plans.

Hamish McHaggis is back in the Underworld where he belongs. Mikey sits on the beach thinking about the one that got away and Claudia rubs goanna liniment into M.I.T.'s aching body.

Meanwhile Nico is out off the break, surfing and arguing with Amycus.

And me?

Well, I've just realised I forgot to pick up Mrs Narrator from the bus-stop. An hour ago!

I'm in big trouble.

Better go.

Cheers.

A GUIDE TO M.I.T.'S* LANGUAGE

1	I hate surfing
0	There's lice in here!
00	I'm too young to die
01	You idiot!
10	I hate sand
11	Bummer
000	Oh,OH!
001	OH, NO!
010	Hello
011	Goodnight
100	Welcome back, goanna-head
101	Pooh!
110	Ouch!
111	ZZZZZ
0000	My yak has fleas
0001	HELP!
0010	Oh, joy
0011	Go away
0100	That's handy
0101	You double idiot
0110	Why me?
1000	Hee hee
1011	His feet stink
1100	What about my TV?
1111	I'm outta here
00000	My head hurts
00001	It's not my fault
00011	That would hurt
00100	This is nice!
00101	This is serious!
00110	The roof is leaking
00111	Hello, ugly!

01001	Hold my hand
01010	Can't make me
01100	Not telling
01110	Bye, bye
01111	GRRRR!
10001	Die, you fiend
10010	Get this smelly lump off me
10101	Just following orders
10111	Panic stations!
11000	Hello, strange animal-headed people
11011	Smarter than you, lizard-brains
11111	HEE HEE HEE
100000	It's only a flesh wound
100011	I want my mummy
100101	Just following orders, fly-breath
100111	Quiet, you stupid animal-headed people
101001	Can't catch me!
101010	Put me down!
101100	Let me go!
101110	What the @%£#$* am I doing here?
110001	You smell, lizard-brains!
110010	Holy Occhilupo, you're ugly
110011	Get your bottom off my leg
110101	Holy Occhilupo!
110110	Gulp!
110111	The whole world's turned dark!
111001	My feet are on fire
111010	I hate water
111011	@%&#$*!!
111100	NNNOOO!
111101	The kettle's boiling
1110111	Yes!

*M.I.T. (pronounced *em-eye-tee*) is short for Mental Image Transfer.

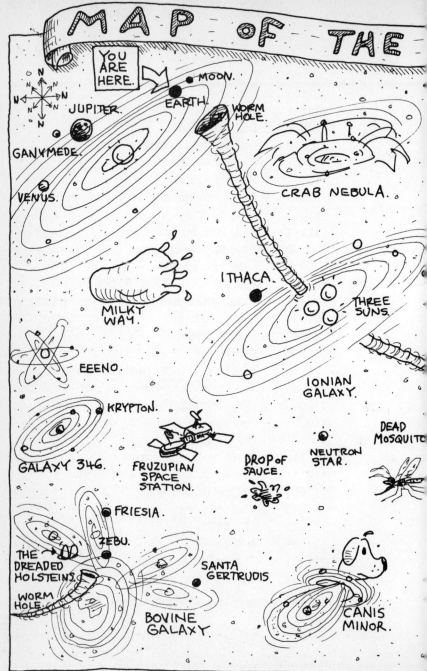

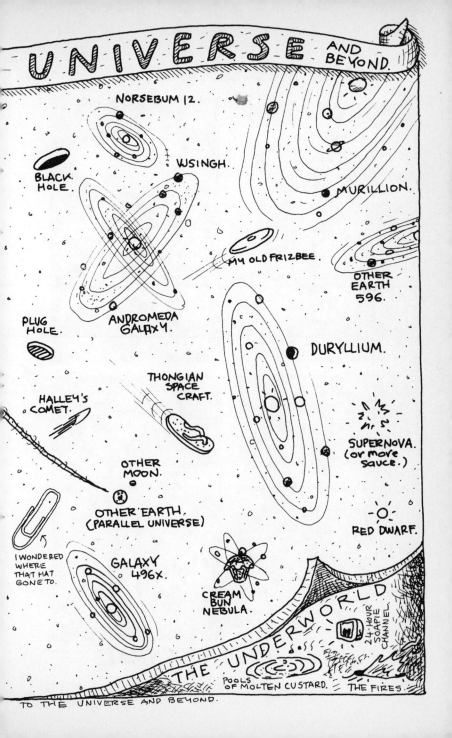

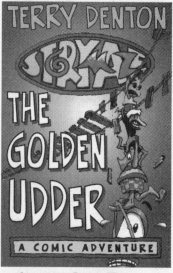